LOVE IS HELL™

A CARTOON BOOK BY MATT GROENING

OTHER BOOKS BY MATT GROENING

SCHOOL IS HELL
WORK IS HELL
CHILDHOOD IS HELL
AKBAR & JEFF'S GUIDE TO LIFE
HOW TO GO TO HELL
THE ROAD TO HELL
THE BIG BOOK OF HELL
BINKY'S GUIDE TO LOVE
THE HUGE BOOK OF HELL

HARPERCOLLINSPUBLISHERS
77-85 FULHAM PALACE ROAD, HAMMERSMITH, LONDON W6 8JB

WWW.HARPERCOLLINS.CO.UK

THIS EDITION FIRST PUBLISHED 2004
1 3 5 7 9 8 6 4 2

ORIGINALLY PUBLISHED IN 1986 BY PANTHEON BOOKS,
A DIVISION OF RANDOM HOUSE, INC., NEW YORK.
COPYRIGHT © 1982, 1983, 1984, 1985, 1986, 2004 BY MATT GROENING

ISBN 0 00 717904 9

PRINTED AND BOUND IN GREAT BRITAIN BY SCOTPRINT, HADDINGTON.

AND NOW, LADIES AND GENTLEMEN, THIS COMIC STRIP TAKES GREAT PLEASURE IN PRESENTING

LOVE IS HELL

BEFORE / AFTER

THE STORY OF (YOUR NAME HERE)

A 13-CHAPTER MINISERIES

BROUGHT TO YOU IN TEENY WEENY EYESTRAIN-O-VISION

THE SLANG OF LOVE

DESPITE MEDIA REPORTS TO THE CONTRARY, ASTUTE LUVOLOGISTS (SCIENTISTS OF LOVE) HAVE POINTED OUT THAT LOVE IS NO COUNTRY HAYRIDE. AS EVIDENCE, THEY OFFER THOUSANDS OF UNDERGROUND STREET TERMS FOR "LOVE." HERE ARE BUT A FEW:

LOOPY
THE TREMORS
JELLY BONES
MUSH-BRAIN
WHIRLORAMA
PALPITATIONS
SLIP 'N' SLIDE
BRICK-IN-THE-FACE
SLOP 'N' MOP
THE GOOEYS
BUCKET-O-CLAMS

WHAT THE GREAT PHILOSOPHERS HAVE SAID VIS-À-VIS LOVE

"LOVE IS A SLIPPERY EEL THAT BITES LIKE HELL." -- BERTRAND RUSSELL

"LOVE IS A PERKY ELF DANCING A MERRY LITTLE JIG AND THEN SUDDENLY HE TURNS ON YOU WITH A MINIATURE MACHINE-GUN." -- KIERKEGAARD

"LOVE IS A SNOWMOBILE RACING ACROSS THE THE TUNDRA AND THEN SUDDENLY IT FLIPS OVER, PINNING YOU UNDERNEATH. AT NIGHT, THE ICE WEASELS COME." -- NIETZSCHE

CHAPTER I:

WHAT IS LOVE?

AND WHAT MAKES YOU THINK YOU DESERVE SOME?

FIG. 1
TYPICAL LOVE MANUEVER

WHOOPS.

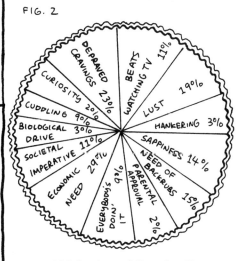

FIG. 2

THE LOVE PIE

(pie chart segments:)
DEPRAVED CRAVINGS 23%
WATCHING TV 11%
LUST 19%
CURIOSITY 2%
CUDDLING 9%
BIOLOGICAL DRIVE 3%
HANKERING 3%
SOCIETAL IMPERATIVE 11%
SAPPINESS 14%
ECONOMIC NEED 2%
NEED OF BACKRUBS 15%
EVERYBODY'S DOIN' IT 6%
NEED OF PARENTAL APPROVAL 2%

LOVE STOPPER'S TEXTBOOK

WATCH OUT FOR THESE EARLY WARNING SIGNS OF LOVE:
BOUNCY STEP
GOO-GOO EYES
BABBLING
BORED FRIENDS

LA LA LA

THE 9-HEADED HYDRA OF LOVE

FIG. 3

SEDUCTION
CRUSH
INFATUATION
OBSESSION
NARCISSISM
UNFOCUSED HORNINESS
DESIRE
INSANITY
FOCUSED HORNINESS
LOVE, LOVE ME DO
TRUE LOVE

WHY YOU MIGHT FEEL UNLOVED:

☐ YOU ARE SUCH A DREADFUL PERSON THAT NO ONE COULD POSSIBLY LOVE YOU.

☐ YOU ARE THE ONLY ONE WHO REALLY EXISTS IN THE UNIVERSE, AND THE REST OF US ARE JUST PHANTOM IMAGES.

☐ WHO THE HELL CARES?

THE SECRET OF LOVE

A SPECIAL NOTE FOR ADVANCED LOVE EXPERTS ONLY:

THE SECRET OF LOVE IS-- WAIT A MINUTE. SOMEONE WHO SHOULD KNOW BETTER IS PEEKING. SO YOU THINK YOU'RE AN ADVANCED LOVE EXPERT, EH? YOU OUGHTA BE ASHAMED.

NEXT: LOVE VS. FREEDOM

© 1984 BY MATT GROENING

A SPECIAL 13-CHAPTER BONUS FUN SERIES! COLLECT 'EM ALL! YOU TO CLIP STRIP, CASE (NOT FOR TAKEN.) UNLESS FORGOT LAST WEEK'S IN WHICH FORGET IT. RESPONSIBLE ADVICE

LOVE IS HELL

CHAPTER II: THE 57 VARIETIES OF LOVE

LOVE MONGER'S TEXTBOOK

AVOID SHARING AFFECTION WITH PEOPLE WEARING DESPERATE T-SHIRTS.

WILL YOU BE MY FRIEND?

IN WESTERN TRADITION, THERE HAVE BEEN APPROXIMATELY FOUR KINDS, OR FLAVORS, OF LOVE. THESE INCLUDE:

1. "PHILIA" FRIENDSHIP, BROTHERLY LOVE — HEY PAL. YO.
2. "EROS" THE DRIVE TO CREATE OR PROCREATE — VOILA. OU.
3. "AGAPE" THE LOVE WHICH IS DEVOTED TO THE OTHER — TRY THESE YUMMY APPETIZERS. OK.
4. "LUST" THE CURRENT FAVORITE — HI PAL. YO.

BUT IN THESE COMPLEX MODERN FINAL DAYS, THE WHOLE CONCEPT OF LOVE HAS EXPLODED LIKE A CORNUCOPIA WITH A STICK OF DYNAMITE STUCK IN IT. THE MESS IS EVERYWHERE. IN FACT, YOU PROBABLY GOT SOME FLICKED ON YOU RIGHT NOW AND YOU DON'T EVEN KNOW IT.

SCIENTISTS WORKING LATE INTO THE NIGHT HAVE NOW ISOLATED SOME 57 VARIETIES OF LOVE. WHAT IS PECULIAR, THEY NOTE, IS THAT MANY OF THESE LOVE-VARIETIES INTERACT SIMULTANEOUSLY, CAUSING MUCH JOY, ECSTASY, CONFUSION, AND FUCK-UPS.

THIS IS CALLED THE "LOVE BLENDER EFFECT"; HENCE THE POPULAR STREET CRY:

I'VE JUST BEEN THROUGH THE LOVE BLENDER!!!

I CAN DIG IT.

WILL YOU BE MY FRIEND.

THE LOVE BLENDER®

DON'T TOUCH THAT DIAL

FRAPPE SHRED PUREE WHIRL REND ASUNDER LIQUEFY

THE 57 VARIETIES OF LOVE

INFATUATION CRUSH STUPEFACTION
PUPPY LOVE FLAME CALF LOVE WHEEE
PLATONIC LOVE ARDOR YEN
PERFECT LOVE WEIRD YEARNING SELF-LOVE WOO
ANIMAL MAGNETISM VEGETABLE MAGNETISM
ITCHY LOVE OBSESSION PURE LOVE YA-YA-YA
DON'T WHAT-THE-HELL LOVE STRONG LIKE
BEE-YOOP BEWITCHMENT SLOPPY LOVE THROBBING LOVE
MMMM BEGUILEMENT BEWILDERMENT
UNSPEAKABLE CRAVING HORNINESS
THUNDERBOLT LOVE OF PASTRIES
PENCHANT FOR SMURF DOLLS BUCKET-O-CLAMS LUST FOR SHOE HORNS
FREE LOVE AC/DC B&D XYZ
HATE HUNGRY-MAN DINNER

PUT THEM ALL TOGETHER AND THEY SPELL

LUV.

NEXT: DATING & MATING & HATING & BERATING

 A 13-CHAPTER CARTOON MINI-SERIES THAT HAS ONLY BEGUN TO FIGHT

CHAPTER IV:
THE 9 TYPES OF GIRLFRIENDS

 LOVESTUMPER'S TEXTBOOK
- WHEN GETTING UNDRESSED WITH A NEW FRIEND FOR THE FIRST TIME, DO NOT TRY TO BREAK THE TENSION BY GESTICULATING WILDLY AND MAKING COMICAL THROAT NOISES.

GEEBA GEEBA GEEBA!

"MS. NICE GUY"

 TICKETS TO THE BOXING MATCH? OH DARLING, YOU SHOULDN'T HAVE.

ALSO KNOWN AS: WHAT A GAL, PRECIOUS, ONE OF THE BOYS, MY MAIN SQUEEZE, DOORMAT.
ADVANTAGES: CHEERFUL, AGREEABLE, KINDLY.
DRAWBACKS: MAY WISE UP SOMEDAY.

"OLD YELLER"

 YOU GODDAMNED SPINELESS GOOD-FOR-NOTHING DRAG-ASS NO-TALENT SON OF A BITCH!!! CAN'T YOU SEE YOU'RE MAKING ME MISERABLE??

ALSO KNOWN AS: SHE-DEVIL, SOURPUSS, THE NAG, MY OLD LADY, WARTHOG FROM HELL.
ADVANTAGES: PAYS ATTENTION TO YOU.
DRAWBACKS: SCREECHES, THROWS FRYING PANS.

"SICKLY"

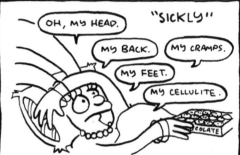 OH, MY HEAD. MY BACK. MY CRAMPS. MY FEET. MY CELLULITE.

ALSO KNOWN AS: WHINER, MEWLER, GLUMPY.
ADVANTAGES: PREDICTABLE.
DRAWBACKS: CONTAGIOUS.

"THE BOSSER"

STAND UP STRAIGHT. PUT ON A DIFFERENT TIE. GET A HAIRCUT. CHANGE YOUR JOB. MAKE SOME MONEY. DON'T GIVE ME THAT LOOK.

ALSO KNOWN AS: WHIPCRACKER, THE SARGE, MS. KNOW-IT-ALL, BALL AND CHAIN, YES MOM.
ADVANTAGES: OFTEN RIGHT.
DRAWBACKS: OFTEN RIGHT, BUT SO WHAT?

"MS. VAGUELY DISSATISFIED"

 I JUST CAN'T DECIDE. SHOULD I SWITCH MY CAREER, GOALS, HOME, AND HAIR COLOR?

ALSO KNOWN AS: THE FRETTER, WORRYWART, TYPICAL, AW CMON HONEY.
ADVANTAGES: EASILY SOOTHED.
DRAWBACKS: EVEN MORE EASILY PERTURBED.

"WILD WOMAN OUT OF CONTROL"

 I'VE GOT AN IDEA. LEZ GET DRUNK N MAKE LOVE ONNA FRONT LAWN. I DONE IT BEFORE. S'FUN.

ALSO KNOWN AS: FAST GIRL, FREEWHEELER, GOODTIME CHARLEENA, PASSED OUT.
ADVANTAGES: MORE FUN THAN A BARREL OF MONKEYS.
DRAWBACKS: UNRELIABLE; DRIVES OFF CLIFFS.

"HUFFY"

I SEE NOTHING HUMOROUS IN THOSE SILLY CARTOONS YOU KEEP SNICKERING AT.

ALSO KNOWN AS: NO FUN, HUMORLESS PRIG, COLD FISH, CHILLY PROPOSITION, ICEBERG, SNARLY.
ADVANTAGES: YOUR FRIENDS WILL FEEL SORRY FOR YOU.
DRAWBACKS: YOU WILL HAVE NO FRIENDS.

"WOMAN FROM MARS"

 I BELIEVE THIS INTERPRETIVE DANCE WILL EXPLAIN HOW I FEEL ABOUT OUR RELATIONSHIP.

ALSO KNOWN AS: THE BABBLER, SPOOKY GIRL, SCREWBALL, LOONY, BAD NEWS, ARTISTIC.
ADVANTAGES: ENTERTAININGLY UNFATHOMABLE.
DRAWBACKS: WILL READ HER POETRY ALOUD.

"MS. DREAMGIRL"

 I AM UTTERLY CONTENT WITH YOU JUST THE WAY YOU ARE, MY HANDSOME GENIUS OF A BOYFRIEND. I THINK WE MUST MAKE LOVE LIKE CRAZED WEASELS NOW.

ALSO KNOWN AS: MS. RIGHT, GODDESS, KNOCKOUT, PERFECTION, GORGEOUS.
ADVANTAGES: FUNNY, INTELLIGENT, UNINHIBITED.
DRAWBACKS: WILL HAVE NOTHING TO DO WITH YOU.

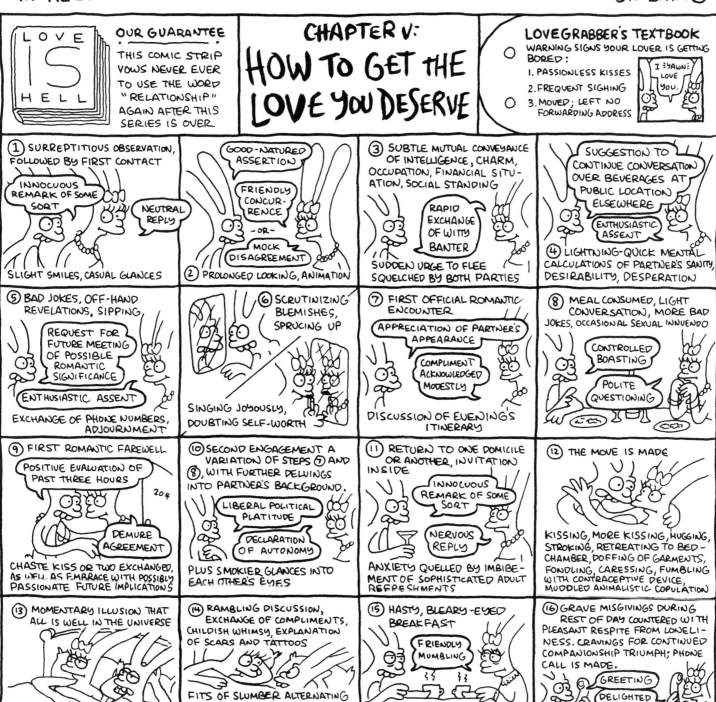

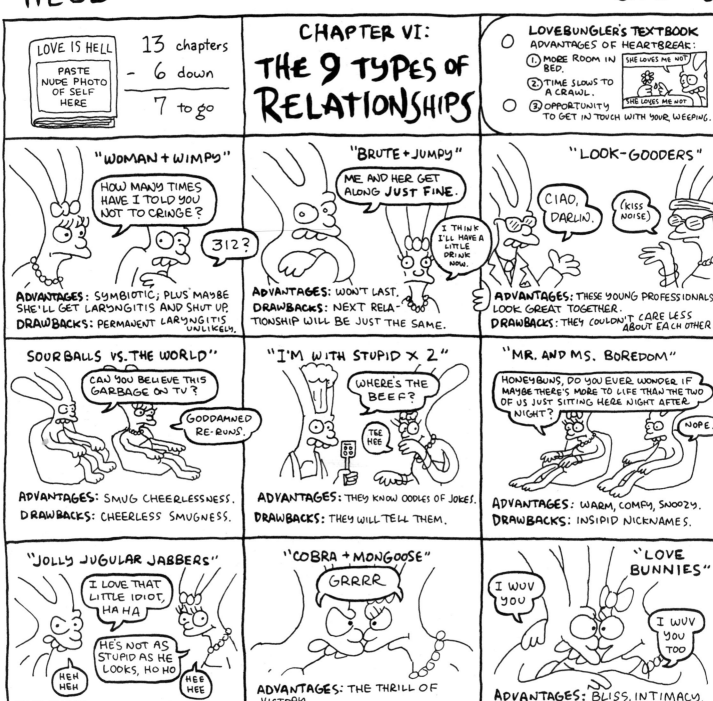

Love is Hell

13 BIG CHAPTERS! 7 DONE! 6 TO GO! OVER THE HUMP!

SOON TO BE A MAJOR UNPRODUCED SCREENPLAY!

CHAPTER VII: DO YOU **REALLY** WANT TO RISK

LOVEMONKEY'S TEXTBOOK

○ WHEN IN DOUBT ABOUT HOW TO PROCEED IN LOVE, HEED THE ADVICE OF YOUR CLOSEST FRIENDS.

○

DON'T LET YER MEATLOAF!!

A SECRET FORBIDDEN ILLICIT TANTALIZING EXOTIC SEXUAL ENCOUNTER WITH A MYSTERIOUS STRANGER?

OR WOULD YOU RATHER JUST READ A CARTOON ABOUT IT?

THE PROS OF LOOSE ANIMALISTIC RUTTING

1. FLEETING MOMENTS OF ECSTASY
2. THE THRILL OF FURTIVENESS.
3. LONELINESS BANISHED FOR AN INSTANT.
4. NEW AND IMPROVED ORGASMS.
5. MIND FREED FROM THINKING ABOUT SEX FOR A FEW MINUTES.

THE MAKING OF THE BEAST WITH TWO BACKS

THIS IS TERRIBLY WRONG

IT'S BAD

OH THE SHAME

IT'S NAUGHTY

FILTHY

DEPRAVED

WE SHOULDN'T BE DOING THIS

CURIOSITY KILLED THE CAT

THE BIBLE FORBIDS THIS

NOT TO MENTION MY DAD

MMM NICE

THE CONS OF FREELY SHARING YOUR LOVE

1. GRUESOME INFECTIONS
2. UNWANTED PREGNANCY
3. BAD REPUTATION
4. PANGS OF GUILT
5. HERPES SIMPLEX
6. HERPES NOT SO SIMPLEX
7. DEPRESSION
8. CHAGRIN
9. SOME WEIRDO DROOLING ON YOU

HINTS FOR HUSSIES

GET DRUNK ENOUGH SO YOU CAN PRETEND YOU DON'T KNOW WHAT YOU'RE DOING

DON'T FORGET!

✓ BRING CONTRACEPTIVES
✓ BE HONEST.
✓ LEAVE A TRAIL OF BREADCRUMBS SO YOU CAN FIND YOUR WAY HOME

SO YOU WANT TO HAVE A SHAMEFUL AFFAIR

YET SOMEHOW YOU CAN'T JUSTIFY IT

THE NEXT TIME YOU ARE CONTEMPLATING A DECISION IN WHICH YOU ARE DEBATING WHETHER OR NOT TO GO FOR THE GUSTO, ASK YOURSELF THIS IMPORTANT QUESTION: **"HOW LONG AM I GOING TO BE DEAD?"** WITH THAT PERSPECTIVE, YOU CAN NOW MAKE A FREE, FEARLESS CHOICE TO DO JUST ABOUT ANY GODDAMNED SNEAKY THING YOUR DEVIOUS LITTLE MIND CAN THINK UP. GO AHEAD. HAVE YOUR FUN. YOU'RE WELCOME. GO ON. SEE YOU IN HELL.

TIPS FOR TOADS

DON'T FORGET THE CLITORIS LIKE LAST TIME, DUMMY

ALWAYS REMEMBER!

✓ S/HE COULD BE A LUNATIC
✓ WHO ARE YOU BETRAYING?
✓ SMILE!!!

20,000,000 B.C. — 1776 — 1945 — YOU ARE HERE — 2001 — 2525 — ETERNITY THIS WAY

LIFESTYLES OF THE RICH AND HELLISH

©1984 BY MATT GROENING

LOVE BE HELL

CHAPTER VIII: SHOULD WE LIVE TOGETHER?

LOVESHOVER'S TEXTBOOK

BE CONSIDERATE. AFTER MESMERIZING YOUR FRIENDS FOR HOURS WITH DETAILS OF YOUR LOVE MISERIES, BE SURE TO FEIGN INTEREST WHEN THEY START BABBLING ABOUT THEIR INSIGNIFICANT PROBLEMS.

SO I GO, "OH YEAH?" AND SHE GOES "YEAH!!" SO I GO--

FUN · INTIMACY · SECURITY · COMFINESS · SHARING CHORES · WAITING TO USE THE BATHROOM · SNUGGLING · NUZZLING · SAYING "HONEY I'M HOME" · GETTING BACK RUBS · GIVING BACK RUBS · GIV--YUCK--FOOT RUBS · DID I SAY NUZZLING? · HAVING HALF AS MUCH SPACE IN THE MEDICINE CABINET · CALMLY DISCUSSING BILLS · WATCHING TV · SHOPPING SENSIBLY · FOLDING BLANKETS TOGETHER · SET...

WHETHER YOU CALL IT COHABITATION, HOLY BEDLOCK, PUTTING ON THE DOUBLE HARNESS, GOING DOMESTIC, HAVING IT RIVETED, OR SHACKING UP, LET'S FACE IT-- LIVING TOGETHER CAN BE THE ADVENTURE OF THE DECADE.

DO I HAVE WHAT IT TAKES TO LIVE WITH SOMEONE?

A WEE TEST

Y N
☐ ☐ I HAVE INFINITE PATIENCE WITH MY PARTNER'S CONSTANT BLUNDERS AND STUPIDITIES

☐ ☐ I CAN GET A GOOD NIGHT'S SLEEP EVEN WITH SOMEONE LYING THERE SEETHING NEXT TO ME

☐ ☐ I AM PREPARED TO PLAY SCRABBLE OCCASIONALLY

LIVING TOGETHER SOLVES PROBLEMS!

✓ IF YOU'RE HYPER, LIVING TOGETHER WILL MELLOW YOU OUT.

✓ IF YOU'RE LONELY, LIVING TOGETHER WILL SOOTHE YOUR HEART.

✓ IF YOU'RE AVERAGE, LIVING TOGETHER WILL LAST 2.3 YEARS.

SIGN UP NOW FOR A LIFETIME OF LIVIN' TOGETHER FUN ACTIVITIES

★ MAKING UP NEW RULES

★ GETTING TOGETHER WITH ANOTHER COUPLE FOR DRINKS

★ POKING GENTLE FUN AT YOUR PARTNER'S SLIGHT WEIGHT GAIN

STILL CONFUSED? THEN ASK YOURSELF THIS SLIMY, SELFISH QUESTION:

"WHY BUY THE LOAF WHEN YOU CAN GET FREE SLICES?"

-- OLD BAKED GOODS PROVERB

OF COURSE, LIVING TOGETHER RAISES NEW QUANDARIES

→ WHAT DO YOU MEAN IT'S MY TURN TO DO THE DISHES?

→ I WAS SNORING?

→ IS IT NORMAL TO MAKE LOVE ONCE EVERY THREE MONTHS?

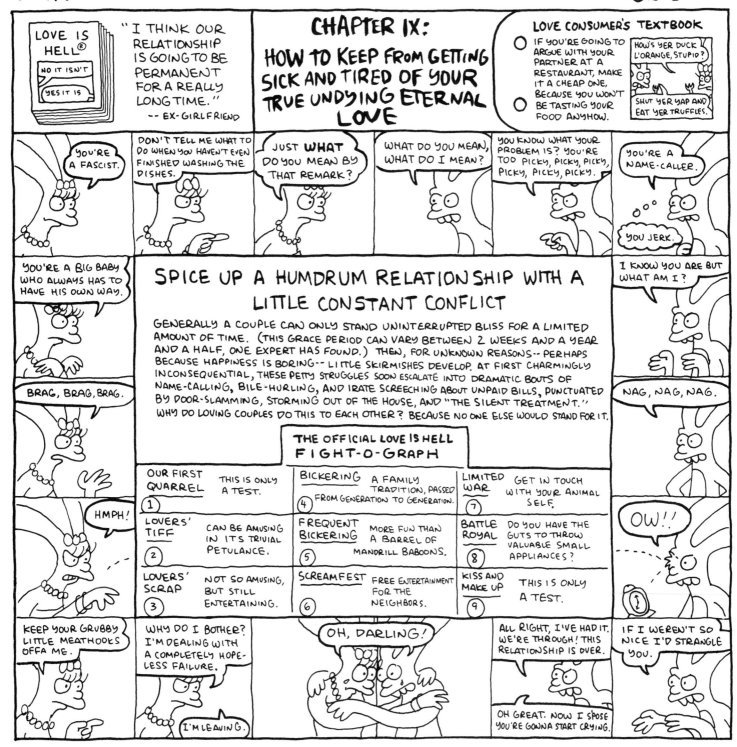

BAT OUT OF HELL

CHAPTER XI:
SPLITSVILLE

LOVESLAMMER'S TEXTBOOK

WHEN HANGING UP ANGRILY ON A LOVER, WATCH THOSE FINGERS!

GO TO HELL!!

SLAM! \\\\\

OW!!!

THE STORY OF A RELATIONSHIP

ONCE UPON A TIME, TWO PEOPLE MET, FELL IN LOVE, AND BEGAN DRIVING EACH OTHER CRAZY.

SOON PETTY BICKERING, BALEFUL STARES, AND DOOR-SLAMMING BECAME THE NORM.

SLAM!!

SLAM!!!

ONE DAY, ONE OF THE PEOPLE GOT FED UP FOR THE LAST TIME, AND SPLIT FOREVER.

LEAVING YOU STRANDED THERE LIKE A BEACHED WHALE.

NOTE: THIS STORY IS ENTIRELY FICTIONAL AND ANY RESEMBLANCE TO INDIVIDUALS LIVING OR DEAD IS PURELY COINCIDENTAL.

HOW TO DUMP YOUR LOVER GENTLY

BE IN A BAD MOOD FOR SEVERAL MONTHS.

CRITICIZE ANYTHING AND EVERYTHING. IF YOU CAN'T SAY SOMETHING MEAN, SAY NOTHING AT ALL.

HONE YOUR JOYLESSNESS.

STOP HAVING SEX.

EAT MEALS IN SILENCE.

WHEN QUESTIONED, REFUSE TO SAY WHAT YOU ARE THINKING.

WHEN THE PROPER MOMENT COMES, LOWER THE BOOM.

THEN SCRAM.

DIVIDING UP THE GOODIES

THAT ZENITH HOME ENTERTAINMENT CENTER IS MINE.

BUT I NEED IT.

THE EXIT RETORT

SLAM!!

YOU'LL BE BACK!!

THE DESPERATE PLEA

PLEASE! DON'T LEAVE ME! I'LL DO ANYTHING!!

GET THE **HELL** OUT OF MY WAY.

DON'T GO YET! I'LL DO MY LITTLE CHARLESTON DANCE!! YOU **LOVE** THAT!

THE WAIT

IF YOU ARE DUMPED

REMEMBER, LIFE WAS ONCE BEAUTIFUL AND FOOD DIDN'T TASTE LIKE CARDBOARD.

PUNCH YOUR PILLOW, NOT THE WALL.

DON'T ACT ON ANY BRIGHT IDEAS YOU SUDDENLY GET, SUCH AS SHAVING YOUR HEAD OR PICKING FIGHTS WITH BURLY THUGS.

DO NOT LOATHE YOURSELF. YOU ARE NO MORE AN UNLOVABLE PATHETIC JERK THAN YOU EVER WERE.

THERE IS MORE THAN ONE CUTTLEFISH IN THE SEA.

DUMPISM DO'S AND DON'TS

WOULD IT BE OK IF I SLEPT OUTSIDE YOUR DOOR TONIGHT? I WON'T MAKE ANY NOISE.

DON'T HUMILIATE YOURSELF.

DO LEARN WHEN TO GIVE UP.

I THOUGHT YOU SAID YOU BROKE UP WITH BINKY.

I BRAKE FOR NO ONE!!

DON'T TAKE YOUR PAIN OUT ON THE REST OF THE WORLD.

DO STEW IN YOUR OWN JUICES.

LOVE. HA. THAT'S A LAUGH.

THE HELL WITH YOU

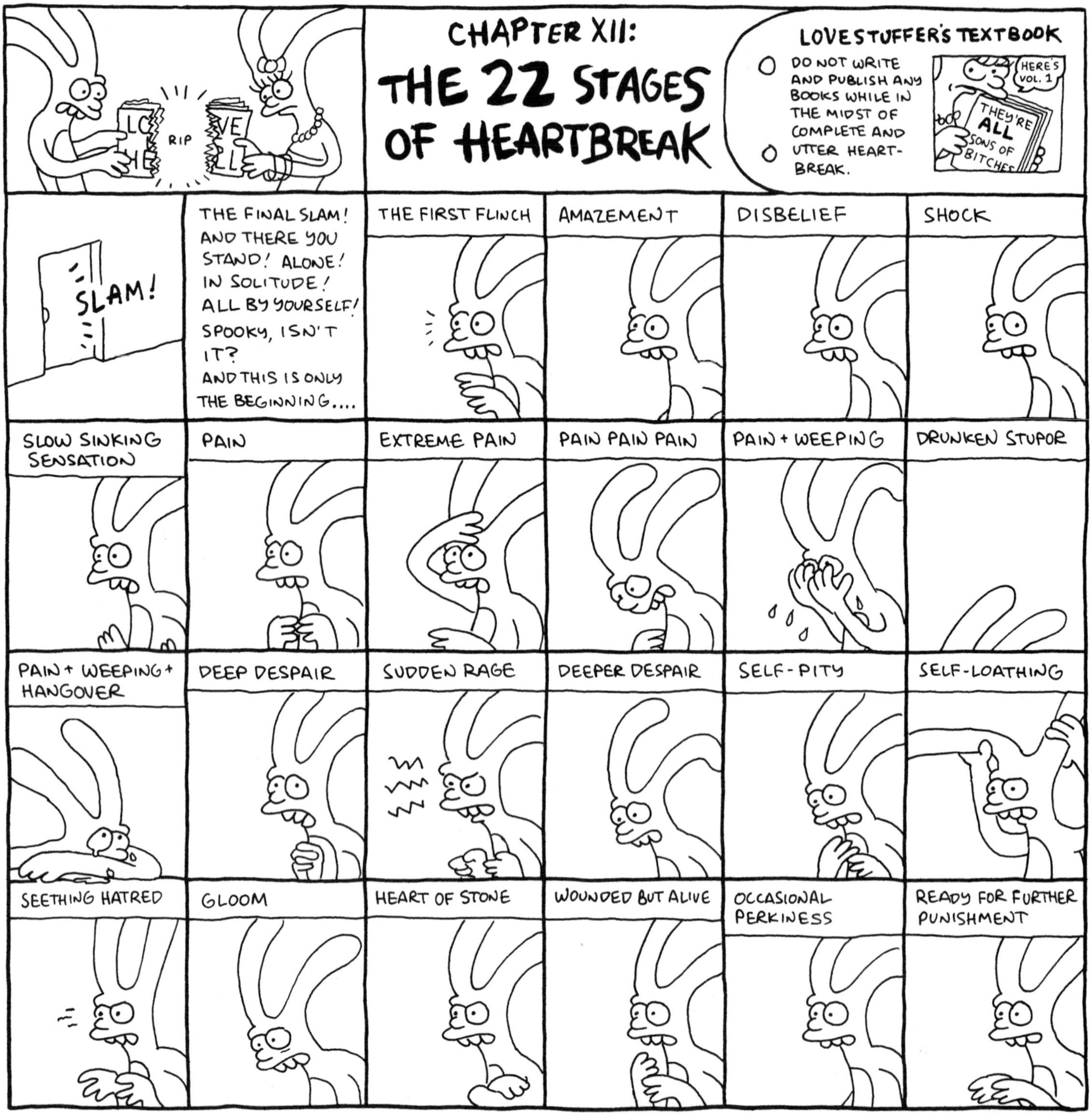

1001 FACES OF YOUR LOVER

THE FOOL

MR. PERFECT

THE WORM

JOE SENSITIVE

BIGFOOT

SEX MACHINE

THE CUDDLER

THE TWO-FACED LIAR

MY DARLING

6 SIMPLE TECHNIQUES TO KEEP YOUR MAIN LOVE RELATIONSHIP ALIVE & KICKING

A PEACEFUL LONG-TERM LOVE-TYPE RELATIONSHIP CAN OFTEN BE LIKENED TO A SLOW BOAT TO CHINA, PUTTERING ALONG THROUGH THE MURKY WATERS NIGHT AFTER NIGHT, MONTH AFTER MONTH, YEAR AFTER YEAR, WHILE YOU AND YOUR LOVE MATEY JUST SIT THERE IN THE BOILER ROOM STOKIN' THE FIRE, CHECKIN' THE PRESSURE GAUGE, OR WATCHIN' CABLE TV. SOUNDS PRETTY BORING, DOESN'T IT? WELL, DON'T DESPAIR -- BY CAREFULLY USING THIS SCIENTIFIC GUIDE, YOU CAN TURN YOUR OWN TEDIOUS LOVE-STEAMSHIP INTO AN ASSERTIVE NUCLEAR-POWERED SUBMARINE OF LUST, EXCITEMENT, AND YELLING.

① PULL A SWITCHEROO.
CONSTANT AFFECTION GETS STALE AFTER A WHILE, SO THE NEXT TIME YOU TALK TO YOUR PARTNER, MIX THE SIGNALS.

> I LOVE YOU, LARD-ASS.

② SHOW CONCERN FOR YOUR LOVER'S SHORTCOMINGS.
THIS TECHNIQUE IS ACTUALLY QUITE GRATIFYING. ALL YOU HAVE TO DO IS SUBTLY POINT OUT YOUR PARTNER'S DEFECTS AND BLUNDERS. AVOID BEING CRUEL WHEN POSSIBLE BY PHRASING YOUR REMARKS IN THE FORM OF PROBING QUESTIONS.

> HOW CAN YOU BE SO STUPID?

③ RESIST THE IMPULSE TO APOLOGIZE.
YOUR PARTNER WILL JUST REALIZE YOU'RE GETTING WEARY, SO YOU'VE GOT TO MAINTAIN YOUR UNYIELDING INTEGRITY. EITHER THAT OR WORD YOUR APOLOGY SO THAT YOU DON'T LOSE FACE.

> YOU BETTER WATCH IT.

> I'M SORRY YOU GOT ANGRY WHEN I CALLED YOU A STUPID LARD-ASS.

④ RECOGNIZE THAT YOUR MATE'S UNHAPPINESS IS NOT YOUR RESPONSIBILITY.
IT'S A DOG-EAT-DOG WORLD OUT THERE, SO WHY SHOULD IT BE ANY DIFFERENT AT HOME? LISTEN PATIENTLY TO YOUR PARTNER'S PROBLEMS, THEN REPLY WITH AN OBJECTIVE SUMMARY.

> YOU KNOW WHAT YOUR PROBLEM IS? YOUR PROBLEM IS YOU'RE PATHETIC.

⑤ REPEAT THE THREE MAGIC WORDS.
SOMETIMES YOU'RE JUST NOT IN THE MOOD FOR A COMPLICATED DISCUSSION WITH YOUR PARTNER. WHEN THIS IS THE CASE, USE THE FOLLOWING THREE MAGIC WORDS TO GET YOUR WAY. YOU MAY HAVE TO REPEAT THE WORDS SEVERAL TIMES, BUT EVENTUALLY THEY **WILL** WORK.

> OH SHUT UP.

⑥ TEMPER YOUR HOSTILITY WITH CLEVERNESS AND HUMOR.
YOU CAN TRANSFORM YOUR NASTIEST FEELINGS INTO MOMENTS OF LEVITY BY COMMUNICATING THEM IN THE FORM OF SUBTLE, WITTY JOKES.

> I DON'T LOVE YOU ANYMORE. JUST KIDDING.

LIFE IN HELL

WHAT NOT TO SAY DURING MOMENTS OF INTIMACY

ARE YOU TRYING TO BE FUNNY?

O MY LORD IN HEAVEN FORGIVE ME FOR THIS VILE SIN I AM ABOUT TO COMMIT.

REMEMBER: I DON'T WANT TO GET INVOLVED.

HAVE YOU GAINED SOME WEIGHT?

WHOOPS-- SORRY.

SHAME ON YOU.

HUP TWO THREE FOUR.

OH LEROY, I MEAN BINKY.

CAREFUL-- DON'T MUSS MY HAIR.

OH MAMA MAMA MAMA.

RING RING

HELLO?

OH NOTHING. WHAT ABOUT YOU?

I LOVE YOU.

OH GOD, LET'S NOT SPOIL IT, OK?

YOU DONE YET?

I FORGOT TO TELL YOU-- I'M LEAVING FOR ALASKA TOMORROW.

OH PAPA PAPA PAPA.

MMM OHH AHH BABY--

ZZZ

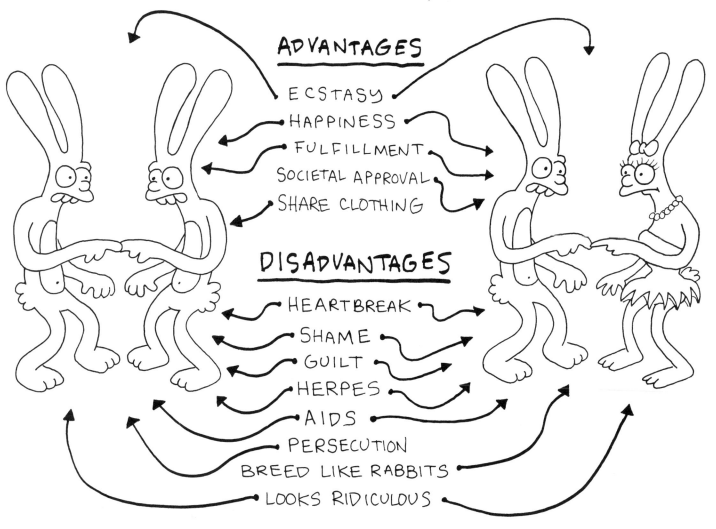

9 SECRET LOVE TECHNIQUES
THAT COULD POSSIBLY TURN MEN INTO PUTTY IN YOUR HANDS

© 1982 BY M. GROENING

WOMEN: MEN! WHAT A WORLD, HUH? IN THE OLD DAYS EVERYTHING WAS EASY, WITH TRUE LOVE AND HEARTS AND FLOWERS AND FRILLY DRESSES AND LIGHT PETTING AND SING-ALONG HAYRIDES -- BUT NOWADAYS EVERYTHING IS SCREWY. YOU ALWAYS GOTTA BE ON GUARD, BECAUSE NO ONE CAN BE TRUSTED -- NOT EVEN YOUR FAVORITE LOVER. IT'S SAD IN A WAY. BUT WE CAN'T JUST GIVE UP. A MAN WITHOUT A WOMAN IS LIKE A TUGBOAT IN A LOGJAM. A WOMAN WITHOUT A MAN IS LIKE A FISH RUN OVER BY A BICYCLE. HENCE THIS HERE GUIDE, TO HELP WOMEN HELP MEN TO SEE THE LOVE LIGHT.

1 DAZZLE 'EM.
FACE IT. MEN ARE DOPES -- GORILLAS -- SWEATY, LUMBERING BEASTS -- AND TO GET THEIR ATTENTION YOU HAVE TO FOOL 'EM -- TRICK 'EM -- PRACTICALLY WHACK 'EM ON THE NOSE WITH A ROLLED UP NEWSPAPER.

HEY -- WHAT FOR YOU WHACK ME ONNA NOSE WITH A ROLLED UP NEWSPAPER?

SAY -- WHAT IS THAT INTRIGUINGLY PROVOCATIVE PERFUME YOU'RE WEARING?

2 FEIGN INTEREST IN THEIR TEDIOUS JABBER.
MEN DIG IT WHEN THEY CAN BABBLE ON ENDLESSLY YEAR AFTER YEAR ABOUT GUNS, BLIMPS, AND CIGARS WITHOUT BEING CHALLENGED TO CHANGE THE SUBJECT. ALL YOU HAVE TO DO IS LEARN A FEW SIMPLE WORDS AND DEVELOP A CAPACITY FOR LENGTHY MONOLOGUES ON CARBURETORS, HOME COMPUTERS, AND CURLY OF THE THREE STOOGES.

RILLY?

MY GOODNESS.

RILLY?

3 ACT PETULANT.
FOR SOME WEIRD REASON, MEN GET A CHARGE OUT OF SEEING WOMEN GETTING REALLY STEAMED -- PARTICULARLY WHEN IT'S ABOUT SOMETHING TRIVIAL, LIKE A RUN IN YOUR STOCKING OR EQUAL PAY FOR EQUAL WORK. JUST STOMP YOUR FOOT ON THE FLOOR, STICK OUT YOUR LOWER LIP, UTTER A LIGHT OBSCENITY, AND LISTEN FOR THAT CONDESCENDING, INDULGENT MALE CHUCKLE THAT SAYS, "WHATSAMATTA, BABY?"

MY YOU LOOK PRETTY WHEN YOU'RE PSYCHOPATHIC.

4 BE UNFATHOMABLE.
ONE THING THAT KEEPS MEN HOOKED IS WHEN THEY CAN'T FIGURE OUT WHAT THE HELL IS GOING ON. THIS IS EASY -- JUST THINK OF YOURSELF AS A FAUCET THAT RUNS BOILING HOT OR ICY COLD WITHOUT WARNING. MEN WON'T LIKE IT, BUT THEY HAVE BEEN KNOWN TO SPEND ENTIRE LIFETIMES TRYING TO UNDERSTAND IT.

I LOVE YOU.

I LOVE YOU TOO.

YOU DON'T KNOW WHAT LOVE IS.

HUH?

PLEASE -- LET'S NOT FIGHT. I LOVE YOU.

5 SLIP INTO SOMETHING A BIT MORE COMFORTABLE.
GET ALL DOLLED UP AND COME ON LIKE GANGBUSTERS. NOTHING CAN SWAY A WOULD-BE DREAMBOAT LIKE RUBY RED LIPS, THREE-INCH PAINTED FINGERNAILS, A PEEK-A-BOO BLOUSE, AND SEE-THRU PANTIES. WORKS LIKE A VOODOO CHARM.

YIKES.

6 ACCEDE TO THEIR SICKO EROTIC REQUESTS.
MEN CAN BE LIKENED TO RUTTING GRIZZLY BEARS, SNURFLING WOLVERINES, OR SEX-CRAZED WHITE RABBITS WITH JUST ONE THING ON THEIR DISGUSTING MINDS. ACTUALLY, YOU CAN PLAY IT TWO WAYS: EITHER FUCK THEIR BRAINS OUT, FOR WHICH YOU WILL BE REWARDED WITH DOGLIKE DEVOTION, OR WITHHOLD ALL SEXUAL FAVORS TILL LATER, FOR WHICH YOU WILL BE REWARDED WITH DOGLIKE DEVOTION.

OOH BABY I LOVE IT WHEN WE CUDDLE.

MMM HMM.

LISTEN MISTER KEEP YER GRUBBY PAWS TO YERSELF.

7 MAKE 'EM WHISTLE A DIFFERENT TUNE.
MEN ARE BASICALLY QUIVERING, SPINELESS JELLYFISH JUST FLOATING ALONG IN LIFE -- BUT WITH THE RIGHT AMOUNT OF PUSHING, PRODDING, AND NAGGING, YOU CAN IMPROVE THEM -- FROM HOPELESSLY INSENSITIVE OAFS INTO HOPELESSLY SENSITIVE OAFS. REMEMBER: KEEP AT IT.

STRAIGHTEN UP, HONEY -- YOU'RE SLOUCHING.

TAKE THAT TOOTHPICK OUT OF YOUR MOUTH. IT'S VULGAR.

YOU'LL THANK ME FOR THIS SOMEDAY.

DON'T GIVE ME THAT LOOK. IT'S UNBECOMING.

8 DEFLATE 'EM.
IT'S SURPRISINGLY EASY TO PUNCTURE THE EGOS OF SLOW-WITTED MALE BEHEMOTHS WITH A QUICK VERBAL JAB OR AN UNYIELDING MORAL/POLITICAL EXHORTATION. CURIOUSLY, MEN FEEL A TREMENDOUS AMOUNT OF GUILT THAT IS HELD IN CHECK ONLY BY AN EQUALLY HEFTY LOAD OF UNFOCUSED RAGE -- AND YOU CAN WORK THIS TO YOUR ADVANTAGE.

HEY LOOK AT THIS SILLY CARTOON.

WHY, IN THIS TIME OF CHANGING VALUES AND FEMALE LIBERATION, DO MEN PERSIST IN LAUGHING AT WOMEN?

I -- I AM FILLED WITH SHAME.

9 PUT YOUR ARM AROUND YOUR HONEY, READ THIS CARTOON ALOUD TOGETHER, AND SAY: "AREN'T YOU GLAD WE'RE BEYOND ALL THIS?"

LIFE IN HE — CALLING ALL MEN! — CALLING ALL MEN!

©1982 BY MATT GROE-NING

9 SECRET LOVE TECHNIQUES WOMEN FIND WELL-NIGH IRRESISTIBLE

FOR MEN ONLY

NO BATTERIES

AS SEEN ON TV

VOID WHERE PROHIBITED

MEN! EVER MEET THAT SPECIAL FEMALE LADY PERSON OF OUR FAIR SEX, THE WOMEN, AND SHE GIVE YOU A LOOK LIKE YOU WAS A WARTHOG FROM HELL? LOTS OF TIMES? WELL LISTEN, BRO, THINGS COULD BE PLENTY DIFFERENT ONCE YOU MASTER THE **9 SECRET LOVE TECHNIQUES WOMEN FIND WELL-NIGH IRRESISTIBLE.** PLENTY DIFFERENT.

SO SETTLE DOWN, TAKE OFF THEM BOOTS, CHOW DOWN ON A HUNGRY-MAN TV DINNER AND A BOTTLE OF LITE BEER, BELCH A COUPLE TIMES, RUB YER FACE, LET OUT A WHOOP, SPIT ON THE FLOOR, AND CHECK THIS OUT.

3. BE MASCULINE!

* MASCULINE = LIKE A MAN

THAT'S RIGHT! MOVE YER ARMS AROUND. FLEX YER MUSCLES. PUFF OUT YER CHEST. STAND UP STRAIGHT. SWAGGER DOWN THE STREET. SQUINT. SNARL. SNEER. MUTTER ANGRY GIBBERISH TO NO ONE IN PARTICULAR. DON'T TAKE NO GUFF.

GRRR

GRUNT

FEH

6. LISTEN AT HER!

UH HUH! NOTHING-- BUT NOTHING--PUTS A WOMAN OFFGUARD LIKE IF SHE THINKS YER PAYING ATTENTION TO HER CEASELESS PRATTLE. MEANWHILES, YOU GOT SOME IMPORTANT THINKING OF YER OWN TO GET DONE -- SO YOU GOTTA LEARN THE SUBTLE GESTURES AND MURMURS THAT'LL KEEP YOU OUT OF HOT WATER! HOO DOGGIES!

MY MY.

HMMM.

IS THAT SO?

WELL AIN'T THAT A CORKER.

1. CLEAN UP YER ACT!

THAT'S RIGHT! TAKE A SHOWER EVERY WEEK AND SCRUB THAT GRIT OFF! THE SMELLY CAVEMAN LOOK SO POPULAR LAST SEASON IS DEFINITELY DÉCLASSÉ NOWADAYS.

WHERZA GURLS?

DON'T BE A DIP-- TAKE A DIP

YUK   YUM

4. COPY HER GESTURES!

YEP! DRIVES 'EM WILD. IF SHE LEANS FORWARD, YOU LEAN FORWARD. IF SHE SCRATCHES HER NOSE, YOU SCRATCH YOUR OWN [IMPORTANT] NOSE. THIS SHOWS YOU ARE BOTH SYNCHRONIZED WITH THE UNIVERSE OR SOMETHING. WORKS LIKE A CHARM.

ARE YOU MOCKING ME?

NO.

HELP! POLICE!

7. GIVE HER THE OLD ONCE-OVER!

NYUP! WHEN A GUY LOOKS A WOMAN UP AND DOWN, FROM THE TOP OF HER NEW PERM TO THE BOTTOM OF HER STILETTO HEELS, IT'S LIKE SAYING, "YOU'RE THE HOSTESS WITH THE MOSTEST!" THIS COURTSHIP RITUAL IS USED THE WORLD OVER, FROM THE LOWLIEST SEA SLUG TO OUR MOST EMINENT BRAINY SCIENCE GUYS.

GOL! SHUCKS! WOO WOO! OOH LA LA! MERCI BEAUCOUPS! IYI YI!

2. GET A NICKNAME!

THAT'S RIGHT! NOTHING PIQUES THE CURIOSITY OF A WOMAN LIKE AN EVOCATIVE NICKNAME. TATOO IT ON YOUR CHEST FOR EASY REFERENCE.

EXAMPLES

"POWERHOUSE"
"MAD DOG"
"ELVIS"
"BIG PEE WEE"
"JANITOR IN A DRUM"

--BUT MY FRIENDS CALL ME "CHUNK-STYLE."

BIG NY

5. PREEN YERSELF BUT GOOD!

THAT'S NO JIVE! WOMEN DIG THAT EXTRA TOUCH THAT TELLS 'EM "THIS GUY IS NIFTY." THINGS LIKE A SPORTY NEW HAIRCUT, BLINKING CHEST MEDALLION, OR HANDY PENCIL TUCKED BEHIND THE EAR. REMEMBER: YOU CAN NEVER USE TOO MUCH AFTERSHAVE LOTION.

HEY. WANNA SEE MY WRIST-CALCULATOR?

BIP BIP

8. SHOW HER WHO'S BOSS!

WATCH OUT! THIS ONE'S A DOOZY, WHAT WITH ALL THE DING-DANG FUSS OVER "EQUALITY," "FREEDOM," AND "JUSTICE." BUT IF YOU STICK TO YER GUNS, JUT OUT YER CHIN LIKE A TOUGH GUY, AND BELLOW "AHH, SHUDDUP" ENOUGH TIMES, SHE'LL GET THE MESSAGE.

REMEMBER: SOME WOMEN ARE EASIER TO FOOL THAN OTHERS.

I SAID GETCHER ASS IN HERE.

WHAT?

OH-- NOTHING.

9. GIVE HER THIS GUIDE, DROP TO YER KNEES, YELP LIKE A WOUNDED PUP, AND SAY: "I GUESS I'M JUST TOO SENSITIVE."

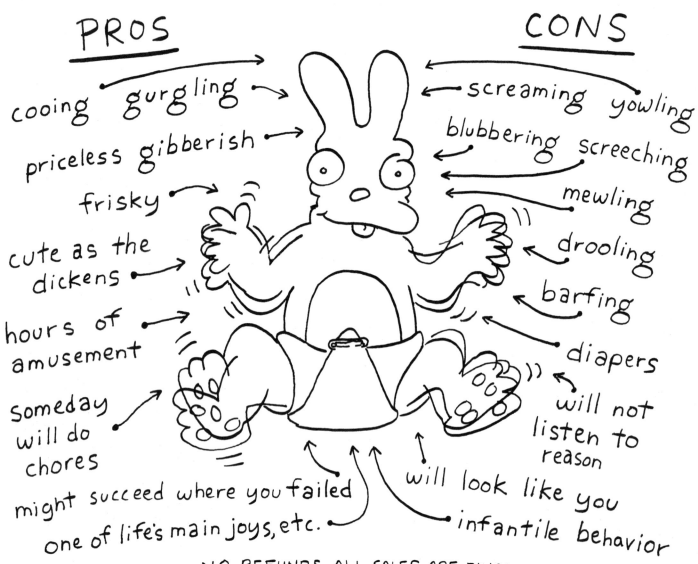

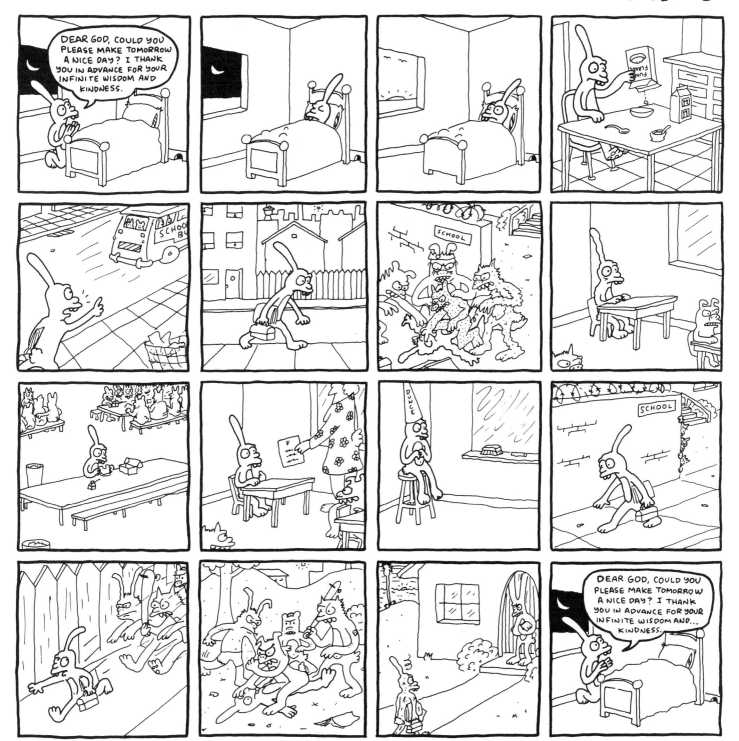

© 1985 BY MATT GROENING

FILE UNDER HELL

OK, SO THERE WAS THIS LADY AND SHE HAD THIS LITTLE PET DOG. AND FOR SOME REASON THE LITTLE DOG'S NAME WAS FREESHOW. OK? SO ONE DAY THE LADY TOOK OFF ALL HER CLOTHES AND SHE WENT INTO THE BATHTUB. SO THE LITTLE DOG SUDDENLY JUMPS OUT THE WINDOW WHEN SHE ISN'T LOOKING, RIGHT? AND SO THE LADY SEES HE'S GONE, AND SHE JUST JUMPS OUT OF THE BATHTUB AND GOES RUNNING DOWN THE STREET, AND SHE'S YELLING "FREESHOW! FREESHOW!"

KIDS' QUESTIONS ABOUT DEATH

WHEN YOU GO TO HEAVEN, DO YOU LOOK LIKE HOW YOU DID WHEN YOU DIED?

IF YOUR LEG GETS AMPUTATED DURING YOUR LIFE, IS IT WAITING FOR YOU IN HEAVEN?

CAN DEAD PEOPLE IN COFFINS HEAR WHAT YOU'RE SAYING?

WELL, HE LIVED A FULL AND REWARDING LIFE, SORT OF.

SURE LOOKS PEACEFUL, DON'T HE?

PLEASE-- SHUT UP-- I BEG OF YOU

IF CATS ARE BAD, DO THEY GO TO CAT HELL?

MEOW

MEOW

MEWL

MEOW

MEOW

ARE THERE CAVEMEN IN HEAVEN?

IF I GO TO HEAVEN, WILL I HAVE ANY FRIENDS?

WON'T ETERNITY GET KIND OF BORING AFTER AWHILE?

WILL I GO TO HELL JUST FOR ASKING THESE QUESTIONS?

LIFE IN HELL

YOUR GUIDE TO THE MODERN CREATIVE ARTISTIC TYPES

CREATIVE ARTISTIC TYPE	DOMINANT PERSONALITY TRAIT	SECONDARY PERSONALITY TRAITS	DISTINGUISHING FEATURES	HAUNTING QUESTION	HOW TO ANNOY THEM
WRITER	SELF-ABSORPTION	POMPOSITY IRRITABILITY WHINING	NERVOUS TWITCHING, BAD POSTURE	"AM I JUST A HACK?"	SAY: BUT HOW DO YOU MAKE A LIVING?
PAINTER	SELF-OBSESSION	DELUSIONS OF GRANDEUR	SPATTERED PANTS, INARTICULATE EXPLANATIONS	"SHOULD I MOVE TO NEW YORK?"	SAY: IT'S NOT FINISHED, IS IT?
POET	SELF-PITY	PARANOIA BITTERNESS BILE	WEIRD LIPS SNIVELING POVERTY	"WHY DOES EVERYONE AVOID ME?"	BE ANOTHER POET.
PERFORMANCE ARTIST	SELF-INDULGENCE	ALIENATION IRRATIONALITY SHAMELESSNESS	VAGUELY PUNKISH LOOK, ONLY WITH WRINKLED SKIN	"GIVEN THE INFINITE NUMBER OF THINGS I COULD DO WITH MY LIFE, WHY AM I STANDING HERE ONSTAGE SLAPPING MEAT ON MY HEAD?"	SAY: I SAW SOMETHING JUST LIKE THAT ONCE ON THE GONG SHOW.
ACTOR	SELF-DEVOTION	SELF-DOUBT	AURA OF INSINCERITY	"DO I HAVE ANY TALENT?"	SAY: PUT ON A FEW POUNDS, HAVEN'T YOU?
ROCK & ROLL GUITARIST	SELF-COMPLACENCY	SLEAZINESS SLIMINESS SMUGNESS	SALLOW COMPLEXION, VENEREAL SCABS	"WHERE AM I?"	THROW BEER BOTTLES AT THEIR HEADS DURING CONCERTS.
STREET MIME	SELF-SATISFACTION	COMPULSION TO PESTER	SCRAWNY BOD TORN LEOTARDS IMPISH BEHAVIOR	"HAVE I NO SHAME?"	PUNCH 'EM IN THE MOUTH.
CARTOONIST	MALICIOUS FRIVOLITY	FRIVOLOUS MALICIOUSNESS	INKY FINGERS INKY SHIRTS INKY PANTS	"WILL I BE DRAWING GODDAMNED RABBITS FOR THE REST OF MY LIFE?"	IT IS UNWISE TO ANNOY CARTOONISTS.

HOW TO BE A CLEVER FILM CRITIC

ARE YOU QUALIFIED TO BE A CLEVER FILM CRITIC?

- ☐ DID YOU HAVE NO FRIENDS AS A CHILD?
- ☐ DO YOU SALIVATE AT THE SMELL OF STALE POPCORN?
- ☐ DO YOU THRILL AT THE PROSPECT OF SPENDING A CAREER WRITING IN-DEPTH ANALYSES OF MOVIES AIMED AT SUBLITERATE 15-YEAR-OLDS?
- ☐ DO YOU MIND BEING LOATHED FOR YOUR CLEVER OPINIONS?

HOW TO PAD OUT A CLEVER FILM REVIEW WHEN YOU DON'T HAVE ANYTHING TO SAY

- ☐ RECOUNT THE PLOT
- ☐ THROW IN GRATUITOUS PUNS
- ☐ WRITE ABOUT YOURSELF

FOR ADVANCED CLEVER FILM CRITICS ONLY!

CAN YOU USE "MISE-EN-SCÈNE" IN A REVIEW THAT ANYONE WILL FINISH READING?

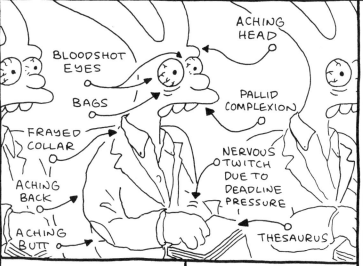

BLOODSHOT EYES
BAGS
FRAYED COLLAR
ACHING BACK
ACHING BUTT
ACHING HEAD
PALLID COMPLEXION
NERVOUS TWITCH DUE TO DEADLINE PRESSURE
THESAURUS

DEVELOP A CLEVER RATING SYSTEM THAT REDUCES YOUR CRITIQUES TO CUTE 'N' EASY CONSUMER GUIDES

☆☆☆ STARS ARE FUN!
9½ NUMBERS ARE IN!
☺☺☺ HOW ABOUT SMILEYS?
$$$ OR DOLLAR SIGNS??

DON'T FORGET CINEMA'S GREATEST PARADOX

THE FRENCH ARE FUNNY.

SEX IS FUNNY.

AND COMEDIES ARE FUNNY.

YET NO FRENCH SEX COMEDIES ARE FUNNY.

CLEVER WORDS TO USE IN REVIEWS SO AS TO ENSURE YOU WILL BE QUOTED IN FILM ADS

PICK ONE FROM COLUMN A AND ONE FROM COLUMN B

COLUMN A	COLUMN B
ADVERBS	ADJECTIVES
RICHLY	HAUNTING
MARVELOUSLY	TOUCHING
WONDERFULLY	ABSORBING
ODDLY	EVOCATIVE
PROVOCATIVELY	COMPELLING
REFRESHINGLY	ELEGANT
STUNNINGLY	ORIGINAL

AND DON'T FORGET THESE HANDY PHRASES:
"I LOVED IT!"
"IT SIZZLES!"
"...GREAT FUN..."
"A MASTERPIECE!"

IF YOU CAN'T BE A CLEVER FILM CRITIC, MAYBE YOU CAN BE:

- ☐ A SNIVELING CINEMA ENTHUSIAST WHO ACTUALLY TRIES TO TALK LIKE A CLEVER FILM CRITIC IN CASUAL CONVERSATION
- ☐ A FILM BUFF SO DEVOTED TO THE MEDIUM THAT YOU HAVE OPINIONS OF MOVIES YOU HAVEN'T SEEN
- ☐ ONE OF THOSE SQUEAKERS WHO WRITES IRATE LETTERS TO CLEVER FILM CRITICS

THE 4 TYPES OF CLEVER FILM CRITICS

WHICH DO YOU ASPIRE TO BE?

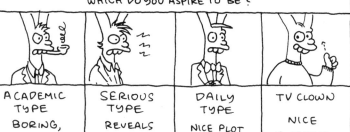

ACADEMIC TYPE	SERIOUS TYPE	DAILY TYPE	TV CLOWN
BORING, UNREADABLE	REVEALS ENDINGS	NICE PLOT SUMMARIES	NICE SWEATERS

LIFE IN HELL
©1985 BY MATT GROENING
THE BRAGGART
TAKE IT FROM ME: DON'T BUY A YACHT
THE GLASSY-EYED LISTENER
I'VE BEEN HAVING THE STRANGEST DREAMS LATELY
THE QUOTER
AS BOB DYLAN ONCE SAID--
THE PATIENT
MY THERAPIST SAYS I'M TOO HARD ON MYSELF. MY THERAPIST SAYS--
THE RESENTFUL SPOUSE
THE CONFESSOR
I HAVEN'T HAD ANY SEX IN--IN--THREE WEEKS.
THE BITTER PILL
I HATE PARTIES
PARTY GAMES
THE LOUD LAUGHER
HAR HAR HAR HAR
THE PROWLER
WHY DON'T YOU DUMP THAT WIMP AND TAKE UP WITH A REAL MAN?
SEARCH & DEVOUR
HOW FAST CAN YOU DEVOUR THE YUMMY APPETIZERS BEFORE THEY'RE ALL GONE?
GUESS WHO
HOW LONG WILL IT TAKE TO REMEMBER THE NAME OF YOUR OLD BUDDY?
HEY BINKY! LONG TIME NO SEE!!
HEY THERE
BILL? FRED? JEFF? JOE? SAM? MOE? ELMER? TIM?
THE ZOMBIE
HI TRIXIE WHAT'S NEW?
MY LIVE-IN BOYFRIEND OF FIVE YEARS DUMPED ME LAST NIGHT
OH
THE CONSPIRACY THEORIST
I TELL YOU THE C.I.A. CONTROLS THE WEATHER
THE ENCHANTED BOX
SEE HOW MANY PEOPLE YOU CAN ANNOY JUST BY TURNING ON THE TV
THE SILENT MARRIAGE COUNSELOR
3.5 MORE MONTHS
MENTALLY CALCULATE HOW LONG BICKERING COUPLES WILL LAST TOGETHER
BATHROOM DETECTIVE
INVESTIGATE THE MEDICINE CABINET
THE OBSERVER
ANYONE EVER TELL YOU YOU'RE LOSING YOUR HAIR?
THE WIT
YOU HEAR THE ONE ABOUT THE STARVING ETHIOPIAN WITH AIDS?
THE AMBIVALENT SEDUCTRESS
NO WAY JOSÉ
COCAINE ADDICT MIND PUZZLER
GO UP TO A COCAINE ADDICT AND SAY:
I'M ONLY GOING TO TELL YOU THIS ONCE. THAT GUY MEL OVER THERE HAS A BUNCH OF COKE WITH HIM, BUT HE'S GOING TO DENY IT. AND I'M GOING TO DENY I EVER TOLD YOU THIS. SEE YOU LATER, PAL.
THE LAST SURVIVOR
SEE HOW LONG YOU CAN LAST BEFORE YOU GET KICKED OUT
THE PARALYZED HOSTESS
MY CARPET
THE DENOUNCER
YOU'RE ALL A BUNCH OF UPTIGHT RIGHT-WING PHONIES
THE PUKER
THE PUNSTER
HIS BARF IS WORSE THAN HIS BITE
THE BABBLER
I WANT TO BE REINCARNATED AS A SEA OTTER
THE MUTUAL WHINERS
IF YOU ASK ME, IT'S THE EMPEROR'S NEW CLOTHES ALL OVER AGAIN
YOU SAID A MOUTHFUL. AND TALK ABOUT OVERRATED--
THE PASSED OUT

© 1985 BY MATT GROENING

HOW TO BE A SENSITIVE POET

HOW TO TELL IF YOU ARE THE SENSITIVE-POET TYPE

YES NO

☐ ☐ ARE YOU "DIFFERENT"?

☐ ☐ DO YOU FEEL "SPECIAL"?

☐ ☐ ARE YOU "COMPLICATED"?

☐ ☐ DO YOU ENJOY "POVERTY"?

YOUR ANSWERS REALLY DON'T MATTER. JUST REMEMBER:

★ IN A COSMIC SENSE, EVERYONE IS A SENSITIVE POET.

★ RECOGNITION ISN'T EVERYTHING.

★ NOTHING IS IMPOSSIBLE.

BEGINNING EXERCISES FOR SENSITIVE POETS

YOU WILL NEED:

PENCIL   PAPER   SOMBER CLOTHING

PRINTED BELOW ARE FIRST LINES OF SENSITIVE POEMS. READ THEM. LET YOUR MIND DRIFT. SET YOUR SOULFULNESS FREE. GO INTO A TRANCE. NOW FINISH THE POEMS.

I SAW A GENIUS IN THE MIRROR TODAY....

ACROSS THE LONELY BEACH I WANDER....

NEAR THE LONELY KNOLL I WEEP....

ON THE LONELY CLIFF I LOITER....

ALAS, THE HORNETS BUZZING IN MY BRAIN....

(BE SURE TO CREDIT THIS CARTOON WHEN YOUR POEMS GET PUBLISHED.)

I SIT IN MY CUBBYHOLE, WAITING, WAITING

I SIT IN MY CUBBYHOLE, WAITING, WAITING, (PAUSE, LOOK STALWART)

SUBJECTS FOR SENSITIVE POEMS

AUTUMN   DEATH PAIN TREES
THE COSMOS CRITICS BEAUTY
CLOUDS SUICIDE DREAMING
LEAVES YOURSELF LONELINESS
FUTILITY BLIGHT DEPRESSION
DECAY LOSS ENTROPY LOVE
FLOWERS BRANCHES TREE STUMPS

DO YOU HAVE THE GUTS TO BE A SENSITIVE POET?

NAY YES

☐ ☐ CAN YOU FACE DISDAIN?

☐ ☐ CAN YOU FACE RIDICULE?

☐ ☐ CAN YOU FACE UTTER INDIFFERENCE?

ADVANCED EXERCISES FOR SENSITIVE POETS

YOU WILL NEED:

PENCIL   PAPER   BITTERNESS

1. WRITE A POEM FROM THE POINT OF VIEW OF A CREAKY OLD BARN (HINT: " I AM A BARN, CREAKING, CREAKING ")

2. WRITE A SONNET ABOUT YOUR MOM.

3. WRITE A POEM ABOUT A FLEETING EMOTION UNIQUE TO YOU, USING A COMPLEX AND PRIVATE SYSTEM OF SYMBOLS THAT NO ONE ELSE CAN POSSIBLY UNDERSTAND.

HOW TO BE A PROFESSIONAL SENSITIVE POET

MISTY VAPORS A POETRY QUARTERLY

SUBMIT YOUR POEMS TO PUBLICATIONS YOU DON'T READ

SUBMIT YOUR POEMS TO PUBLICATIONS THAT DON'T PRINT POETRY

FISHIN' ILLUSTRATED

 CULTIVATE A SNEERING HATRED OF ALL OTHER SENSITIVE POETS

AND REMEMBER: WHEN IN ELKVILLE, BE SURE TO STOP BY THE TOMB OF THE UNKNOWN SENSITIVE POET AND SET A SPELL.

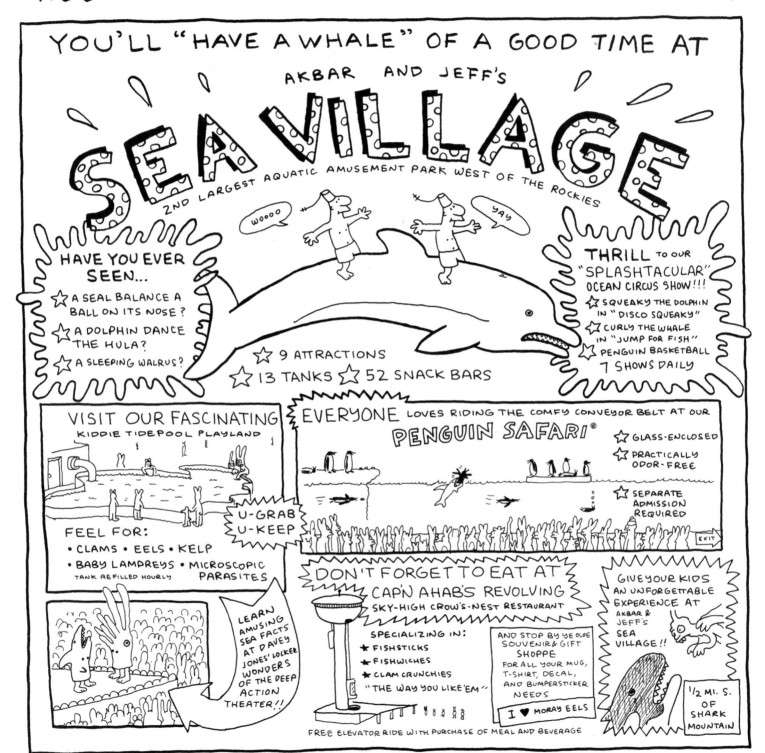

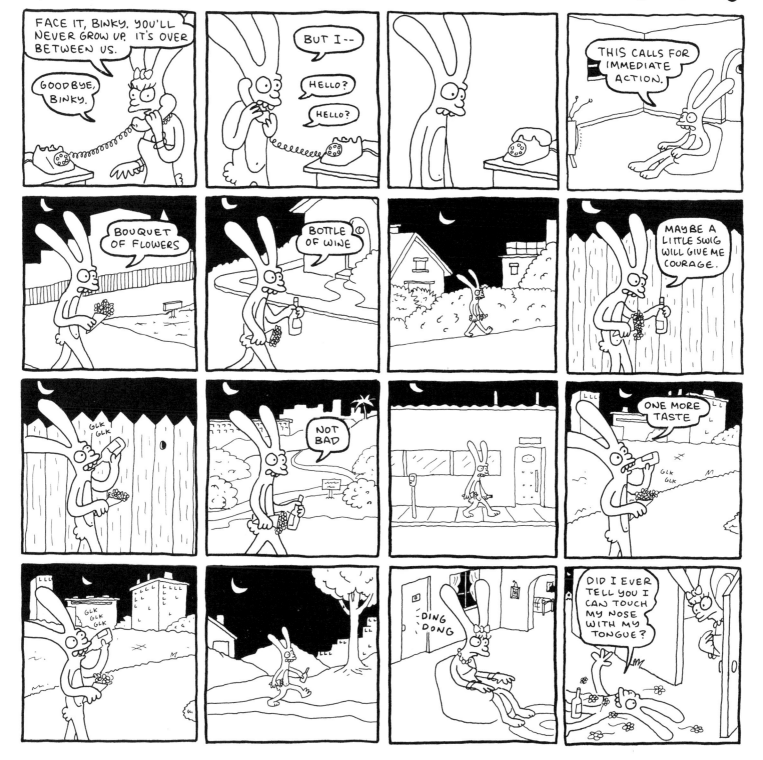